D0820843

by Natalie Lunis

Consultant: Jonathan G. Way
Author of *Suburban Howls*
www.EasternCoyoteResearch.com

NEW YORK, NEW YORK

Credits

Cover, © Exactostock/SuperStock and © Bev McConnett/iStockphoto; TOC, © Design Pics/SuperStock; 4–5, © Leonard Lee Rue III/Photo Researchers, Inc.; 6, © Twildlife/Dreamstime; 7, © Jianchun/Dreamstime; 8, © John Shaw/BCI/Photoshot; 9, © Tom & Pat Leeson; 10, © George McCarthy/Nature Picture Library; 11, © age fotostock/SuperStock; 12T, © Rich Kirchner/NHPA/Photoshot; 12B, © S & D & K Maslowski/FLPA/Minden Pictures; 13, © W. Perry Conway/Aerie Nature Series; 14T, © Minden Pictures/SuperStock; 14B, © George McCarthy/Nature Picture Library; 15, © Minden Pictures/SuperStock; 16T, © Tom & Pat Leeson; 16B, © Daniel J. Cox/Natural Exposures; 17, © Flirt/SuperStock; 18, © S & D & K Maslowski/FLPA/Minden Pictures; 19, © Thomas Kitchin & Victoria Hurst/First Light/Alamy; 20T, © Steve and Dave Maslowski/Maslowski Wildlife Productions; 20B, © age fotostock/SuperStock; 21, © Panoramic Images/Getty Images; 22, © Royalty Free Composite and Panoramic Images/Getty Images; 23TL, © Leonard Lee Rue III/Photo Researchers, Inc.; 23TM, © age fotostock/SuperStock; 23TR, © Jianchun/Dreamstime; 23BL, © George McCarthy/Nature Picture Library; 23BM, © W. Perry Conway/Aerie Nature Series; 23BR, © Tom & Pat Leeson.

Publisher: Kenn Goin
Editorial Director: Adam Siegel
Creative Director: Spencer Brinker
Cover Design: Dawn Beard Creative and Kim Jones
Photo Researcher: Picture Perfect Professionals, LLC

Library of Congress Cataloging-in-Publication Data

Lunis, Natalie.
Coyote : the barking dog / by Natalie Lunis ; consultant: Jonathan Way.
p. cm. — (Animal loudmouths)
Includes bibliographical references and index.
ISBN-13: 978-1-61772-279-0 (library binding)
ISBN-10: 1-61772-279-0 (library binding)
1. Coyote—Juvenile literature. I. Title.
QL737.C22L86 2012
599.77'25—dc22

2011005277

For more information, write to Bearport Publishing Company, Inc., 45 West 21st Street, Suite 3B, New York, New York 10010. Printed in the United States of America in North Mankato, Minnesota.

070111
042711CGB

10 9 8 7 6 5 4 3 2 1

Contents

Howling Together

It is nighttime in the woods.

A few short, squeaky yips and yaps come from a coyote somewhere in the distance.

Soon more yipping and yapping starts up in another spot.

Before long, other voices join in, and the yips turn into howls.

The sounds seem to come from ten different coyotes, all in different places.

Coyotes usually howl in the early evening after it gets dark, at night, or early in the morning.

Playing Tricks with Sound

Are there really ten coyotes howling in the woods?

No—the sound of a large group is coming from only four or five animals.

Howling coyotes are able to change how high or low their voices are.

They can also change the loudness or softness of their howling.

By playing with sound in this way, one **pack**, or family of coyotes, can make itself seem bigger and tougher.

A pack of coyotes is usually made up of an adult male and female and their young—some of which are full-grown and as big as their parents. The pack howls to warn other packs to stay out of its **territory**.

Many Meanings

Sending a warning message to other packs isn't the only reason coyotes howl.

Sometimes a coyote howls to check in with other members of its pack and let them know it is safe.

Other times a coyote howls to bring the whole pack together.

Coyotes also make other kinds of sounds with other meanings.

They bark to warn other pack members of danger.

They growl and snarl to scare off animals that come too close.

coyote growling

The coyote's scientific name—*Canis latrans*—comes from Latin words meaning "barking dog." In fact, coyotes are wild members of the dog family, as are foxes and wolves.

Places to Call Home

Coyotes live in most parts of North America and in some parts of Central America.

They can survive in different kinds of **habitats**, including forests, deserts, and **prairies**—and even in towns and cities near people.

Some of these places have cold, snowy winters, and some are warm all year long.

In fact, coyotes can live anywhere that they can find places to hide, stay safe, and hunt for food.

Coyotes in the Wild

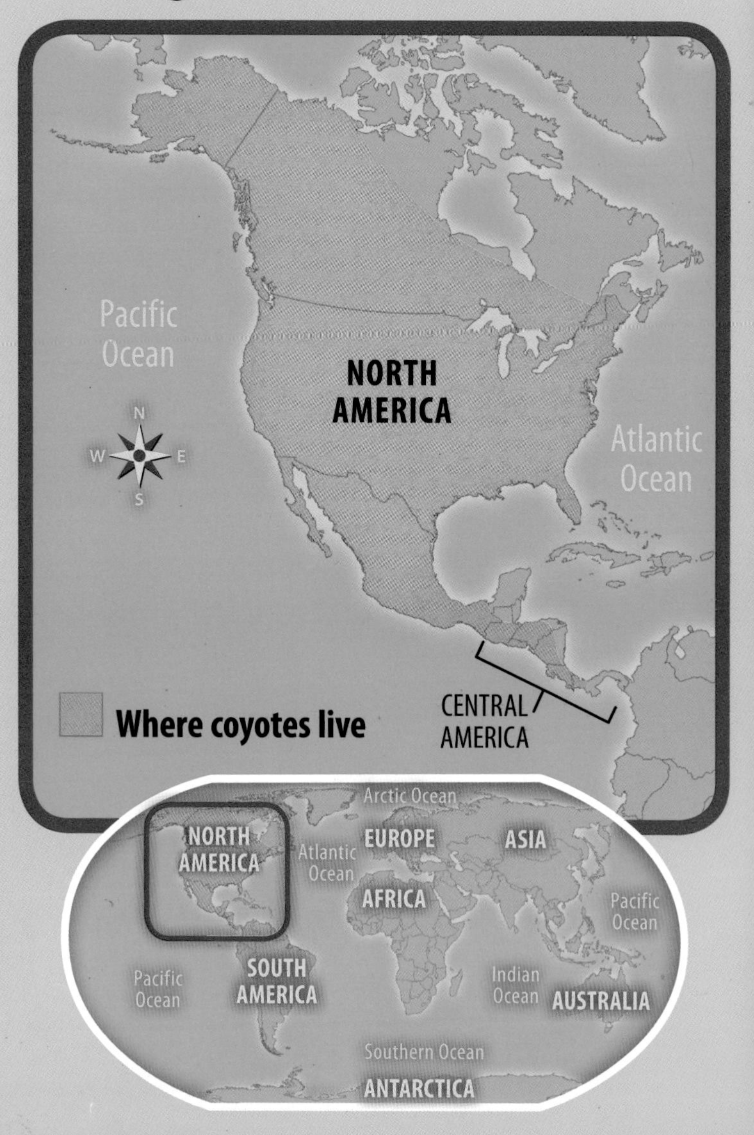

coyote on a prairie

Coyotes live in every U.S. state except Hawaii.

coyote in a desert

Hunting Small Animals

Coyotes usually sleep during the day and hunt at night.

They catch mainly small and medium-size animals such as mice, rats, rabbits, gophers, woodchucks, and young deer.

They use their sharp senses of sight, smell, and hearing to find the creatures.

Often, when a coyote is close enough to attack its **prey**, it freezes in place—then it pounces and quickly grabs its meal.

Other times it has to chase its prey before catching it.

coyote pouncing on a mouse

Coyotes measure about 25 inches (.6 m) tall at the shoulder and weigh 20 to 30 pounds (9 to 14 kg)—though some in the eastern United States get up to 50 pounds (23 kg).

mouse

Hunting Big Animals

When coyotes go after mice and other small animals, they often hunt on their own or in pairs.

Sometimes, however, pack members work as a team to hunt larger animals, such as adult deer or elk.

Usually they pick out an animal that is weak because it is very old, young, or sick.

The coyotes take turns chasing the animal to tire it out.

Then they attack and kill it—eating quickly in case other animals come by and try to take their food away.

elk

deer

Coyotes do not eat only meat. They eat just about any food they can find, including nuts, berries, and other fruit.

coyotes eating elk

Playful Pups

Baby coyotes, called pups, start learning to hunt when they are about ten weeks old.

Before that, they drink milk from their mother's body and eat food that their parents bring them.

As the pups grow bigger and stronger, they playfully bite and pounce on one another.

They do this to practice the skills they will need to catch animals.

When they are about six months old, the young coyotes are ready to hunt and find food on their own.

pups drinking their mother's milk

pups playing

Pups yip, yap, and start to howl. As they do, they are practicing the sounds they will need to **communicate** with other coyotes.

Spreading to Cities

In recent years, coyotes have begun spreading to most towns and cities in the United States.

There, they can find mice and other small animals to eat, along with food scraps in garbage cans.

Unfortunately, coyotes that live near people can cause problems.

Sometimes they attack pet dogs because they think the animals are in their territory.

Sometimes they attack and even eat cats.

Los Angeles, Chicago, Boston, and New York are a few of the many cities where coyotes have been spotted.

Living with Coyotes

Living with coyotes in towns and cities isn't always easy, but there are many things people can do to prevent problems.

For example, they can keep their cats indoors, especially at night, and always walk their dogs on leashes.

They can also keep garbage cans tightly closed.

Doing these things is a good idea.

After all, coyotes are here to stay—so it's best to try to get along with them.

Because the noisy animals are able to survive in many different kinds of places, their howls will be heard for a long time to come.

coyote eating dog food left outside

Coyotes rarely attack people. When they see a person, they are usually afraid and run away. In fact, there are only about three to five coyote attacks on people each year in the United States.

Sound Check

Scientists measure how loud or soft sounds are in units called decibels. A coyote's howl measures about 90 decibels. That's about the same as the noise made by a gas-powered lawn mower. The chart below shows how this level of loudness compares to some other sounds.

Whisper
20 decibels

Normal Speaking Voice
60 decibels

Coyote or Gas-Powered Lawn Mower
90 decibels

Train Engine
115 decibels

Ambulance Siren
120 decibels

Airplane Taking Off
140 decibels

Glossary

communicate (kuh-MYOO-nuh-kayt) to pass on information, ideas, or feelings

habitats (HAB-uh-*tats*) places where animals live and find everything they need to survive

pack (PAK) a group of at least three coyotes

prairies (PRAIR-eez) large areas of flat land covered with grass

prey (PRAY) an animal that is hunted and eaten by other animals

territory (TER-uh-*tor*-ee) an area of land that belongs to and is defended by an animal or a group of animals

Index

Read More

Marsico, Katie. *How Do We Live Together? Coyotes (Community Connections).* Ann Arbor, MI: Cherry Lake Publishing (2010).

Mattern, Joanne. *Coyotes Are Night Animals (Night Animals).* Milwaukee, WI: Weekly Reader (2007).

Webster, Christine. *Coyotes (Backyard Animals).* New York: Weigl (2008).

Learn More Online

To learn more about coyotes, visit
www.bearportpublishing.com/AnimalLoudmouths

About the Author

Natalie Lunis has written many science and nature books for children. She lives in the Hudson River Valley, just north of New York City.